# Supporting THE DECISION TO JOIN

### What Association Boards Should Know and Do About Membership and Affiliation

**JAMES DALTON**   ASAE & THE CENTER FOR ASSOCIATION LEADERSHIP

asae & the center™
for association leadership

WASHINGTON, D.C.

The author has worked diligently to ensure that all information in this book is accurate as of the time of publication and consistent with standards of good practice in the general management community. As research and practice advance, however, standards may change. For this reason it is recommended that readers evaluate the applicability of any recommendations in light of particular situations and changing standards.

ASAE & The Center for Association Leadership
1575 I Street, NW
Washington, DC 20005-1103
Phone: (202) 626-2723; (888) 950-2723 outside the metropolitan Washington, DC area
Fax: (202) 220-6439
Email: books@asaecenter.org
We connect great ideas and great people to inspire leadership and achievement in the association community.
Keith C. Skillman, CAE, Vice President, Publications, ASAE & The Center for Association Leadership
Baron Williams, CAE, Director of Book Publishing, ASAE & The Center for Association Leadership

Cover design by Beth Lower, Art Director, ASAE & The Center for Association Leadership
Interior design by Troy Scott Parker, Cimarron Design

This book is available at a special discount when ordered in bulk quantities. For information, contact the ASAE Member Service Center at (202) 371-0940.

A complete catalog of titles is available on the ASAE & The Center for Association Leadership website at www.asaecenter.org.

ISBN-13: 978-0-88034-310-7
ISBN-10: 0-88034-310-9

Printed in the United States of America.

10 9 8 7 6 5 4 3 2 1

# Contents

*Introduction*  v

Chapter **1 Perceptions of Membership Benefits**  1

Chapter **2 The Value of Member Involvement**  7

Chapter **3 How Leaders' and Members' Perceptions Differ**  15

Chapter **4 Generational Differences and Similarities**  25

Chapter **5 The Quest for International Status**  37

*Closing Thoughts (Including Board Exercise)*  45

*Additional Reading and Programs*  51

*About the Author*  53

# *Introduction*

A S A BOARD MEMBER, your fiduciary responsibilities include keeping close watch on the association's balance sheet to ensure that expenses not only align with the budget but also reflect strategic priorities. On the other side of the balance sheet, you're looking for steady streams of income, one of which is typically membership dues. When membership numbers grow and remain strong, the association is well-positioned to fund programs, activities, and initiatives to further advance its mission.

If your association depends upon dues to provide a substantial percentage of its annual income, then membership recruitment and retention have the power to make—or break—the budget. Simply understanding why someone joins and remains a member of your association can help you be a more effective volunteer leader.

In 2006, to further that understanding, ASAE & The Center for Association Leadership, in Washington, D.C., conducted a study of why professionals do (or do not) join an association. The comprehensive study pooled data from the member and nonmember databases of 18 diverse professional associations, forming a survey population large enough to generate more than 16,000 responses. By its design, the study set aside differences among doctors, engineers, accountants, and court reporters to homogenize all 18 disciplines and identify the way "professionals" consider the membership decision.

The study's results, published in *The Decision to Join* (2007, ASAE & The Center for Association Leadership), reveal a striking similarity in how professionals, no matter what their occupation, think about association membership. Consequently, the data provide a baseline for comparison, so your association can determine the extent to which the profession it represents differs from a class of people collectively known as "professionals."

In addition, the large survey response invites a statistically valid look at membership segments—such as those under a certain age or with fewer years of experience in the profession—that typically constitute too small a response population when one association surveys its membership. For example, *The Decision to Join* study allowed for a valid comparison between those who have served in a governing capacity with those who are under 30 years of age and have not yet become active in the association in a meaningful way. These segment comparisons offer insights that associations may never be able to explore in their own member surveys.

## 5 Key Points

From the many findings presented in *The Decision to Join*, several emerge as having significant relevance for volunteer leaders in governing roles. Those are summarized in this publication, which is written specifically for association board members with the intent of deepening their understanding of how their responsibilities relate to member expectations.

In some cases, these findings will confirm your association's own research and assumptions. In other cases, however, they may defy conventional thinking and provide new insights on the membership challenges that your association faces.

Based on the findings, here are the five points that especially warrant board members' attention:

**1. Focus more on the collective benefits of membership, less on the personal benefits.** An association serves as a "cooperative" for professionals, a place where they share information and personal energy; these customers are not only willing to give but also expect to receive. Although this unique proposition leads to products and services, marketing the association as merely a provider of those outcomes diminishes its most distinctive asset. In fact, *The Decision to Join* study shows that most professionals understand and appreciate that association membership helps them fulfill an obligation to advance the common good of their profession.

**2. Define, encourage, and measure member involvement.** When asked about the value they receive from membership, members who are involved in associations give staggeringly different responses compared to those who are not involved. Yet the simple act of performing one task, on one occasion, is all it takes to change a member's disposition toward the value of membership. With involvement, loyalty builds. Without it, energy and positive perceptions dissipate.

**3. Don't assume that elected leaders can correctly identify the priorities of rank-and-file members.** Although elected by their peers, volunteer leaders quickly gain a vantage point unknown to most other association members. The leaders have access to unique intelligence sources and information that put considerable distance between the conclusions they reach and the assumptions under which rank-and-file members operate. The association must take steps to understand members' needs and preferences or risk setting strategic priorities that do not resonate with most members.

**4. Stop worrying so much about the younger generation.** Younger professionals may be masters at social networking, texting, and blogging, but that prowess doesn't mean they don't value many aspects of association membership. In fact, they're not as different from baby boomers as you might think.

**5. If the association plans to go global, first square up with domestic members.** Before trying to figure out if international professionals will join your heretofore American association, find out if existing members will revolt when they do. Launching a global strategy without fully analyzing its driving motives or ultimate objectives can alienate domestic members.

The following pages explore each of these points in greater depth. You'll also find the applicable data that support them; for more detailed results, please refer to *The Decision to Join,* available at www.asaecenter.org/bookstore.

CHAPTER **1**

# Perceptions of Membership Benefits

MORE THAN ONE HISTORIAN has remarked that the once-powerful American railroads stumbled badly when they failed to realize they were in the transportation business. That observation represents the difference between knowing what you do (the producer-oriented view) versus understanding the value you provide (the customer-oriented view).

Associations may be making the same mistake as the railroads, especially if their marketing materials offer bulleted lists of what the association does—such as providing advocacy and offering educational opportunities—rather than explaining the value members receive. Even those associations that solely "sell the sizzle," by translating products and services into the visceral qualities that the customer experiences by making a purchase, may be off the mark. This strategy, while undeniably effective for marketing for-profit products and services, is based on a straightforward producer-to-consumer business transaction. But that's not the business model in the association field.

By its very nature, an association must balance "what's in it for me" with "what's in it for us." In other words, members accrue benefits both individually and collectively. Personal benefits are akin to what the for-profit world sells—the tangible goods and services received as a function of membership. Other benefits advance "the good of the order"—they are the products and services from which everyone in the profession receives value, regardless of membership status. As an example, a portion of a profession may pay association dues to advocate a public policy position; the benefits accrue to everyone, including those who don't (or won't) pay for the advocacy.

## What's Really Important?

To explore the effects of this bifurcated value proposition, *The Decision to Join* research included 20 statements that describe the benefits typically offered by a full-service association. Eight of them describe personal benefits, and 12 address benefits to the overall field. Using a scale of 1 to 5 (5 = very important), survey respondents were asked to rate the importance of each benefit to their decision to join the association.

# Importance of Association Benefits

*Rated on a 1-5 scale with 5 = very important.*

| Personal Benefit | Mean Importance Rating |
|---|---|
| Access to the most up-to-date information available in the field | 4.22 |
| Professional development or educational program offerings | 3.91 |
| Opportunities to network with other professionals in the field | 3.72 |
| Access to career information and employment opportunities | 3.39 |
| Access to products, services, and suppliers | 3.21 |
| Opportunities to gain leadership experience | 3.05 |
| A reference directory of members/practitioners | 2.93 |
| Member discounts or group purchasing activities | 2.85 |
| **Mean Importance Index*** | **3.40** |

* Average importance rating for all variables in this group.

| Benefit to the Field | Mean Importance Rating |
|---|---|
| Providing standards or guidelines that support quality | 3.85 |
| Gathering, analyzing, and publishing data on trends in the field | 3.77 |
| Maintaining a code of ethics for practice | 3.74 |
| Promoting a greater appreciation of the role and value of the field among practitioners | 3.70 |
| Conducting research on significant issues affecting the field | 3.70 |
| Promoting greater public awareness of contributions in the field | 3.67 |
| Influencing legislation and regulations that affect the field | 3.64 |
| Supporting student education and entry into the field | 3.58 |
| Attracting competent people into the field | 3.53 |
| Certifying those who meet critical competency standards | 3.52 |
| The association's role in defining critical competencies | 3.44 |
| Providing awards or recognition for excellence in the field | 3.07 |
| **Mean Importance Index*** | **3.63** |

* Average importance rating for all variables in this group.

As shown in the "Importance of Association Benefits" table, the personal benefit statements collectively received a 3.40 rating, while the benefits to the field were rated at 3.63. Given the large size of the respondent population, this seemingly small variance constitutes a statistically significant difference. In short, the benefits for the good of the order are more important than personal benefits, though both hang closely together—as a good balancing act should.

Furthermore, the end result is similar when the findings were cross-tabulated to look at respondents who are currently members of an association versus former members or those who were never members of an association. The good of the order is still more important to former members, although the gap between the scores is a bit narrower when compared to current members. Interestingly, when asked why they dropped their membership, former members did not place less value on the collective benefits of belonging. Rather, they did not believe the association delivered effectively enough on those benefits to the field.

Those who have never been members of any association balance the two types of benefits in near parity, but the nod still goes to the common good. To the extent this "never a member" segment is slightly biased by a prevalence of younger people, the survey also finds that younger people tend to acquire a stronger appreciation for the common good as they mature (See Chapter 4, Generational Differences and Similarities).

Based on the data, the personal benefits and the benefits to the field represent the Yin and the Yang of association membership. The two types of benefits are the complementary opposites on a spectrum of value.

*"I have often admired the extreme skill with which the inhabitants of the United States succeed in proposing a common object for the exertions of a great many men and in inducing them voluntarily to pursue it.*

*Thus the most democratic country on the face of the earth is that in which men have, in our time, carried to the highest perfection the art of pursuing in common the object of their common desires and have applied this new science to the greatest number of purposes."*

— Alexis de Tocqueville, *Democracy in America* (1835)

# Recommendations

- Ensure that your association balances benefits to individual members and to the profession as a whole. While members of professional associations desire and appreciate personal benefits, they also understand that professionalism carries an obligation to support and promote the common good.

- Don't let anyone market the association as a mere provider of products and services. Positioning the personal benefits of association membership just like a product or service in the for-profit sector is akin to promoting the weaker half of the value package.

- To increase the percentage of younger people who join your association and remain members, consider educating them on the value of the common good.

CHAPTER **2**

# The Value of Member Involvement

THE UNIQUE APPEAL OF association membership is not simply based on the combination of personal benefits and benefits to the field. The research findings confirm that members get something else out of membership by becoming involved in the association.

Now, before reading any further, take a few moments to answer this question: What percentage of your membership is actively involved in the association? To estimate this accurately, assume that "actively involved" refers to anyone who has contributed to the work of the association during the last year, in any capacity. Do not include those who participated in an event, such as conference attendees. For now, keep the estimate in the back of your head.

When making your estimate, you acknowledged the distinction between participation and involvement. The latter means sweat equity—putting effort into accomplishing an activity. To determine the impact of such voluntary service on the perception of value received from an association, this study compared four populations of respondents:

- **Governance level:** those who reported serving on the national or local board or on an administrative committee.

- **Committee level:** those who reported serving on any type of program committee.

- **Ad hoc level:** those who participated in at least one task that added value for the association (as opposed to an appointed position that typically requires an extended commitment).

- **Nonparticipants:** those who have not served in any capacity for at least the last year.

A marketing analysis tool known as the Net Promoter Score was used to compare these populations. Developed by Fred Reichheld and described in his book *The Ultimate Question* (2006, Harvard Business School Press), the Net Promoter Score is determined by asking customers one simple question: "How likely is it that you would recommend our (association) to a friend or colleague?" Respondents express their answers on a 10-point scale and are then categorized into three groups: Promoters (9–10 rating), Passives (7–8 rating), and Detractors (0–6 rating). Note that the standard for Promoter status is rather high, including only ratings of 9 and 10.

Although you might consider an 8 as a pretty good score on a 10-point scale, Reichheld's research led him to conclude that an 8 is merely a Passive rating. The concept behind this is, in a sense, egocentric. When asking for recommendations, other people are essentially asking you to stake your reputation on something that someone else does. Prudent people are inclined to hedge their bets. Otherwise, if you give something an excellent rating and the inquiring person has a negative experience with it, your credibility in evaluating the quality of the product or service is called into question. So you might preface a recommendation by saying, "Well, it worked well for me, but I had only one encounter with it." That would be a passive remark.

On the other hand, giving something a 9 or a 10 rating shows that your confidence in the item and your loyalty to the provider are high enough for you to put your name at risk. To determine the Net Promoter Score, you simply subtract the Detractors from the Promoters and drop the Passives out of the equation.

# Higher Involvement, Higher Marks

When asked, "How likely is it that you would recommend membership in [name of association] to a friend or colleague?" here's how the respondents answered based on their levels of involvement:

**Level of Involvement**

| | Governance | Committee | Ad hoc | Not involved |
|---|---|---|---|---|
| Promoters | 65.8% | 60.7% | 46.8% | 39.6% |
| Passives | 21.7% | 27.2% | 33.6% | 31.8% |
| Detractors | 12.5% | 12.1% | 19.6% | 28.6% |
| **Net Promoter Score** | **53.3%** | **48.6%** | **27.2%** | **11.0%** |

Predictably, respondents' perception of the value they receive from membership increases with their level of involvement in the association. In fact, those involved at the governing and committee levels are much alike in their Promoter and Net Promoter Scores. But note the difference between the not involved and the ad hoc groups. The latter includes those who performed one simple task, and the data indicate that doing just one thing for the association nearly triples the Net Promoter Score. A little sweat equity appears to be very powerful stuff.

## The Power of Personal Suggestion

*The Decision to Join* survey also asked respondents how they first learned about their association and provided 15 possible answers, including direct mail, Internet searching, and talking to colleagues. Nearly 80 percent of the respondents said they first learned about their association through some form of face-to-face communication. For example, more than one third of respondents (34.1 percent) learned about the association from a colleague or co-worker, while 26.2 percent had a professor or instructor provide the introduction. All other media fell into the background of secondary significance.

These findings appear to support the often-cited power of first impressions. A member's initial awareness of an association is apt to be what someone else says about it—and what that other person has to say carries a lot of weight.

Let's return to your estimate of members actively involved in your association. Does it fall somewhere between 10 and 15 percent? That's the range in which the vast majority of association leaders typically place their estimates.

Based on the survey results, here's how respondents described their level of association involvement.

**Respondents by Level of Involvement**

| | | |
|---|---|---|
| Board/Administrative | 6.8% | **14.6%** |
| Program Committee | 7.8% | |
| Ad Hoc | | **15.5%** |
| No Involvement | | **69.9%** |

With 14.6 percent of respondents reporting involvement at the board/administrative and program committee levels, an estimate between 10 and 15 percent would be good guesswork on anyone's part—except for one critical factor. That 14.6 percent includes only members officially appointed to do things for the association. It doesn't include the small army of people engaged in ad hoc activities—such as submitting or reviewing journal articles, making presentations at meetings, or even collecting tickets at a banquet—who represent another 15.5 percent of members. Lifting an elbow in any such manner seems to have a considerable impact on loyalty to the association and on members' willingness to risk their reputation when asked about it.

In retrospect, *The Decision to Join* survey failed to ask one important question: "Would you be willing to help your profession by doing something for the association?" Some associations that have asked this question in their own membership surveys have registered "yes" answers from upwards of 80 percent of respondents. When asked the follow-up question of "Why haven't you been involved in the association?" many of those willing volunteers had a ready response: They had never been asked.

## Recommendations

- Define specific levels of involvement, and invite all members to participate in some way. Make it easy for them to accept the invitation to help, no matter what the depth of involvement. The extent to which people say they are willing to be involved might be greater than your association has imagined.

- Develop a database of ad hoc tasks that members can perform without making the greater commitment that a committee or board appointment would entail. Encourage association leaders to refer to the database and then invite new or uninvolved members to "discover the professional value of networking" by lending a hand and meeting some colleagues. Performing just one simple task can increase a member's satisfaction with the association.

- Assemble the names of ad hoc volunteers into a second database to facilitate further communication, including thank-you notes and inquiries about additional involvement. This would not only improve the productivity of the association but also represent a conscious effort to cultivate a larger group of loyal members, or Promoters.

- Develop a performance metric for volunteer involvement. Because members are much more satisfied with the association when they provide input in the form of voluntary work, increased involvement may correlate with higher membership retention and increased membership.

- Given how much face-to-face communication among colleagues influences the decision to join, develop a means of tracking and cultivating members who are Promoters by virtue of their willingness to recommend the association to others.

# CHAPTER 3

# How Leaders' and Members' Perceptions Differ

A S NOTED IN CHAPTER 2, members' perception of the value received from an association rises substantially with their increasing levels of involvement. According to the study, something else rises as well—the likelihood that elected leaders will see issues and priorities differently than rank-and-file members. In extreme cases, volunteer leaders may no longer be in sync with those who elected them.

This can be a difficult proposition to accept. After all, elected leaders are also members and, for the most part, they work alongside colleagues who are not involved in (or not even members of) the association. Those grassroots connections provide leaders with a solid grasp of what the rank-and-file wants, needs, and thinks. The leaders were elected to bring the members' perspective into the association's decision-making process, and that's what they do. At least, that's what associations tell themselves as a reason for not conducting a lot of customer research. Problem is, that conclusion doesn't square with the research results.

## Significant Disparities

Several differences emerge in the area of value propositions when comparing survey responses for elected leaders (the 6.8 percent of respondents who serve on a governing board) with responses from the rank-and-file (the noninvolved members who represent 69.9 percent of respondents). The two groups assign significantly different values for several personal benefits and benefits to the field, as shown in the table on the next page.

In the personal benefits category, two value propositions show a significant difference: networking opportunities and opportunities to gain leadership experience. In both cases, the elected leaders rank the value proposition higher than the rank-and-file. In fact, executive leadership ranks networking opportunities at the top of its list of personal benefits, while rank-and-file members rank it third. As for opportunities to gain leadership experience, there's little wonder why volunteer association leaders rank that higher on their list of personal benefits (fourth) than rank-and-file members (seventh).

In the category of benefits to the field, elected leaders rank two value propositions higher than rank-and-file members. Leaders' top benefit is promoting

# Ranking Membership Benefits by Leadership Role

| Personal Benefits | Elected Leadership | Rank-and-File Members |
|---|---|---|
| Opportunities to network with other professionals in the field | 1 | 3 |
| Access to the most up-to-date information available | 2 | 1 |
| Professional development or educational program offerings | 3 | 2 |
| Opportunities to gain leadership experience | 4 | 7 |
| Access to career information and employment opportunities | 5 | 4 |
| Access to products, services, and suppliers | 6 | 5 |
| A reference directory of members/practitioners | 7 | 6 |
| Member discounts or group purchasing activities | 8 | 8 |

| Benefits to the Field | Elected Leadership | Rank-and-File Members |
|---|---|---|
| Promoting a greater appreciation of the role and value of the field among practitioners | 1 | 4 |
| Providing standards or guidelines that support quality | 2 | 1 |
| Maintaining a code of ethics for practice | 3 | 2 |
| Influencing legislation and regulations that affect the field | 4 | 7 |
| Promoting greater public awareness of contributions in the field | 5 | 6 |
| Supporting student education and entry into the field | 6 | 8 |
| Certifying those who meet critical competency standards | 7 | 9 |
| Gathering, analyzing, and publishing data on trends in the field | 8 | 3 |
| Attracting competent people into the field | 9 | 11 |
| Conducting research on significant issues affecting the field | 10 | 5 |
| The association's role in defining critical competencies | 11 | 10 |
| Providing awards or recognition for excellence in the field | 12 | 12 |

a greater appreciation of the role and value of the field (ranked fourth by rank-and-file members). Leaders also place more value on influencing the legislation and regulations that affect the field (ranked fourth versus seventh).

On the other hand, elected leaders rank two collective benefits *lower* than rank-and-file members: gathering, analyzing, and publishing data on trends (ranked eighth by leaders versus third by rank-and-file members); and conducting research on significant issues affecting the field (10th versus fifth).

Although the survey findings do not explain the reasons behind these disparities, several hypotheses come to mind.

*Networking opportunities.* Do the leaders possess some inherent difference that pulls them toward these benefits? Or have the majority of members simply not yet discovered the full value of these association benefits? At the least, both populations rank networking among their top three benefits, indicating the overall need to emphasize this membership benefit.

*Leadership opportunities.* By ranking this benefit seventh out of eight, the rank-and-file may be indicating they are simply unaware of its potential value. In that case, promoting leadership opportunities would be worth the effort.

But the disparity could be pointing out the classic difference between needs and wants. If customers want something, meaning they see its value, then the marketer simply makes them aware of the brand's availability and competitive advantage. If customers need something, but don't appreciate that fact, then the marketer faces the more difficult task of converting a need to a want. In effect, marketing becomes a two-phase sales project: first sell the need, then sell the service.

For example, one professional association's research revealed that clients of its members thought the profession needed to be more assertive in advocating on their behalf. This information gave the association clear evidence that their members needed leadership training. Unfortunately, members failed to sign up for the training programs to address this need. Convincing members that they need leadership development requires a very different message than the standard marketing copy that simply describes the wonderful features of a leadership program.

*Promoting a greater appreciation of the field's role and value.* This often involves dealing with border disputes among collaborating professions. Accounting for the disparate rankings of this benefit may be a simple matter of adrenalin. Rank-and-file members rank it fourth out of 12 benefits to the field, indicating they believe the issue is important but don't necessarily want to address it themselves. Of course, it falls to the elected leaders to don the war paint, assume diplomatic airs, and square off with another profession's leadership. If you are the leader engaged in what can be stressful deliberations, your insider role may affect your perception of the benefit's importance.

*Influencing legislation and regulations.* The different rankings can probably be attributed to the intelligence and perspective that leaders gain by virtue of their office. Staff and outside experts brief them on all of the issues affecting the profession, and they engage in discussions about possible long-term consequences. In contrast, rank-and-file members remain more focused on the here and now; a narrower set of issues affects their part of the profession's environment. And in some cases, it's possible that leaders have become so insulated from adversities experienced by the rank-and-file that the association does not adequately address them.

*Conducting research and gathering/disseminating data on trends.* The other two disparities in the benefits to the field category may represent the flip side of the intelligence-gathering advantage enjoyed by leadership. Leaders may be so well briefed that they take for granted all the statistics and data they have; they assume others enjoy the same access to information. Rank-and-file members have fewer information-gathering functions at their disposal and therefore place greater importance on conducting research and publishing information on trends affecting the field.

Many associations have ceded such market analytics efforts to commercial publications in their field, thus jeopardizing their position as the most credible information source in the industry or profession. Once lost, this position is difficult to regain. Associations that think doing so isn't worth the effort may

## Quantifying the Differences

In *7 Measures of Success* (2007, ASAE & The Center for Association Leadership), a research team adapted the matched-pair methodology used by Jim Collins in his bestselling book *From Good to Great* and applied it to associations. When measured against merely good associations, great associations exhibited seven attributes.

One of these attributes, being data-driven, refers to an association's propensity to be a market research organization. A data-driven association doesn't depend on elected leaders' knowledge of the profession and their colleagues as its only means of knowing the customer. Rather, a data-driven association seems to know instinctively that elected leaders and members aren't always in sync, so it uses multiple means to continuously track and evaluate members' needs and preferences.

A similar example comes from the for-profit sector, where Proctor and Gamble constantly conducts research on its customers. As one P&G executive reportedly said, "When you can estimate what your customer thinks 85 percent of the time, your competitive advantage lies in going after that 15 percent of your blind area."

need to check with their grassroots network and/or conduct market research on the very subject of market research. The disparity of rankings may indicate sheer ignorance on the part of elected leaders of what is really important to the members/customers.

Overall, as summarized in Chapter 1, the survey respondents placed more importance on the benefits to the field than on personal benefits of membership. And, while this difference is statistically significant, the overall ratings are close enough to emphasize the need to sell members on both personal benefits and benefits to the field.

Interestingly, the difference widens considerably when the data are cross-tabulated by elected leaders and rank-and-file members. The latter still put more emphasis on benefits to the field than on the personal ones, but by a smaller margin than elected leaders do. That means elected leaders may tend to allocate more resources for the good of the order—in other words, benefits to the entire field—than might be warranted by other members' needs and preferences.

## Recommendations

- Don't assume that elected leaders are in sync with rank-and-file members on all matters. Collect data to understand where and why the groups may have disparate views.

- When detecting that elected leaders are out of sync with other members—a knowledge that takes systematic inquiry, not gut instinct—develop a communication plan to explain why elected leaders made a certain decision and then test to find out if the explanatory messages are getting through.

- As a planning and budgeting exercise, classify the association's programs into the two benefit categories. Compare the resource allocations between personal benefits and benefits to the field and, if significant differences emerge, discuss the implications.

CHAPTER 4

# Generational Differences and Similarities

GENERATION X… GENERATION Y… Millennials… Whatever you call the younger generations, you've probably heard a lot about them in the context of membership. According to conventional wisdom, these younger generations no longer find value in the association experience, which will lead to marked declines in the sizes and influence of membership organizations.

Much of this concern is fueled by the popularity of categorization schemes that assign unique psychographic characteristics to generational age groupings—for example, Generation Y is so proficient at networking online that they may never join an association with Internet capabilities that are primitive by their standards. This approach marks each generation with an identity tag that remains for life; because every generation is different, each future generation will require deciphering and tagging.

Generational categorization is at odds with a more traditional classification system that assumes people acquire distinct needs as they move through age-related phases of development. The former focuses on permanent characteristics that influence preferences for life, while the latter looks more at needs that change across time in a fairly predictable manner (for example, starting a career, reaching the top of the career ladder).

Is it true that associations are facing a lost generation or the end of membership as it has been known for eons? Certainly, people under the age of 30 are not joining associations at the same rate as people older than 30, which means that the under-30 age group is significantly underrepresented in many associations. This demographic reality raises another question: Is the current cyber-generation of young people characteristically different in the way they see associations, or has every under-30 age group been slow to join associations?

Depending on the answer to this question, two very different strategic scenarios come into play. If the current cohort of young people is indeed different and permanently less inclined to join associations (the generational model), they may already see associations as lumbering anachronisms, out of touch with their needs and riding into yesterday like an Oldsmobile. Still, some believe it's not too late to mitigate this dire fate. They advise considerable research into the unique needs of this generation, followed by substantial investments in completely retooling the association's product and service line.

The second scenario assumes that the younger generation will grow into membership as its members enter the stages that associations have traditionally focused on and served fairly well (the career stages model). If this seems a bit too complacent—effectively saying, "Stay cool and let them come to us"—the more assertive option has associations acknowledging the probability of age bias in the programs they offer and working harder to serve the entry-level needs that the younger age group has always had. This, too, requires research into career-stage needs, possibly followed by some tweaking of how products and services are designed, promoted, and positioned.

## Maturing into Membership

In 2006, Arthur C. Brooks of Syracuse University conducted one of the more thorough studies of generational differences as they are apt to affect the decision to join an association. The results of Brooks' study, *Generations and the Future of Association Participation* (2006, SmithBucklin Corporation), not only negate the first scenario's assumption that inherent differences will incline younger generations to bypass association memberships but also clearly document the second scenario's premise that entry-level age groups are simply slow to join.

Brooks cites the Social Capital and Community Benchmark Survey (SCCBS) undertaken in 2000 by a researchers' collaboration with the Roper Center for Public Opinion Research and the Saguaro Seminar at Harvard University's Kennedy School of Government. At that time, Generations X and Y had significantly lower association membership rates than the Baby Boomers, which could be construed to support the notion that the younger groups are inherently different. He points out, however, that the Generation X respondents were between 25 and 35 years of age in 2000. Four years later, Brooks conducted a similar study that confirmed most of the SCCBS findings—except for one notable exception. The four-year time lapse had moved most of the Generation X population past the age of 30, and they had surged ahead of the Baby Boomers in terms of their association membership.

This finding led Brooks to conclude, "Generation X and Y workers show great promise to join associations as they move into their peak earning years. Correcting for race, gender, education, political views, religious beliefs, marital status, and family size, the data reveal that Generation X and Y workers are not inherently less likely than Baby Boomers to join associations. On the contrary, given rising incomes and improving job opportunities, young workers show every indication of joining associations at even higher rates than the Baby Boomers, more than making up for their slightly smaller numbers. The bottom line is that fear over the effects of Generation X and Y on association membership is not warranted."

While the Brooks study was retrospective in that it looked back at the joining behaviors of young professionals as they moved into their 30s, *The Decision to Join* study took a prospective approach. It asked two related questions, one dealing with respondents' current estimation of the value received from associations and the other projecting this value into the future. As shown in the table below, responses to the here-and-now question show an age-sensitive progression.

**What is your overall attitude toward associations?**
*% "very favorable" on a 5-point scale, with 5 = very favorable*

| | |
|---|---|
| Under 30 years old | 30% |
| 30-42 | 32% |
| 43-59 | 37% |
| Over 60 | 43% |

In this snapshot, the perception of association value clearly increases with age. It moves from a modest level of appreciation on the younger side of the spectrum to much more favorable sentiments as the respondent population matures.

Here's how the different-aged populations responded when asked to look five years into the future:

**Will there be a greater or lesser need for associations five years from now?**
*Percent "greater need" on a 3-option scale: greater, lesser, about the same*

| | |
|---|---|
| Under the age of 30 | 42% |
| 30-42 | 38% |
| 43-59 | 37% |
| Over 60 | 38% |

When predicting the future value of associations, the youngest generation surges ahead to take the lead position by a significant margin. What could account for this? The idea of five years into the future may carry different connotations for each age group. For the oldest, the relevance of an association probably declines with the prospects of retirement. So the age group that gives associations the highest estimations of value here-and-now drops into parity with the next two age groups. Respondents in their mid 40s and 50s may see or already be at the peak of their careers, which may have a moderating effect on their five-year appraisal of association value. Those between the ages of 30 and 42 predict a greater need for associations in a percentage equivalent to the two older groups; this may indicate that "the future" begins to homogenize and flatten out for all once they have reached a certain age.

The youngest age group presents a different profile. (The size of the respondent database—more than 16,000—makes this difference statistically significant.) For those under the age of 30 to see a much greater need for associations when they look five years into the future indicates a surge in awareness, which corresponds to the surge in memberships found in the Brooks study once young professionals moved from their mid-20s into their 30s.

In Brooks' retrospective analysis, associations have greater appeal for people as they move toward completion of their entry-level career phase. In this prospective study, the perception of future needs indicates a similar phenomenon. All age groups settle into a common view of the future, except for the youngest population. It's as if those under 30 suddenly realize that the future poses challenges that may warrant a little help from some friends, who can be found in the form of an association.

## Youngest Express Most Dissatisfaction

Discovering by age 30 that associations might provide much-needed career development assistance doesn't mean that the youngest age group has the same needs as professionals in other career stages. In fact, when compared with all other age groups, respondents under the age of 30 differ significantly in their view of these personal benefits:

*Access to the most up-to-date information available in the field.* All age groups ranked this as the most important personal benefit. The youngest respondents, however, were the only age group to report a negative performance gap. In other words, when asked to express their satisfaction with the association's delivery of up-to-date information, the youngest members registered the most dissatisfaction.

Perhaps the youngest group's lack of long-term perspective leaves them without the context needed to understand the information they are receiving. Or maybe younger members don't believe their associations communicate in timely and technologically efficient ways. In either case, younger members do not view associations as being "up to date."

*Professional development or educational program offerings.* All age groups ranked this as the second most important personal benefit, with the youngest group giving this benefit a higher "very important" rating compared to their older colleagues. Again, those under the age of 30 were the only group fundamentally dissatisfied with their association's performance in delivering this benefit.

One possible explanation is that, traditionally, the cost of delivering professional development has biased this activity toward the older groups having lower levels of need but better access to resources to pay for education and travel expenses. Internet delivery of this activity may provide an opportunity for associations to improve their perception of value among this age group, assuming that accessibility is the issue. On the other hand, if younger members are taking issue with the content delivered by the association, then an in-depth educational needs analysis is needed.

*Access to career information and employment opportunities.* The youngest age group ranked this third on their list of eight personal benefits, compared to fourth on the lists compiled by the next two older groups (and seventh on the list of those over the age of 60). And, once again, those under the age of 30 are the only respondents who give their association a negative performance rating.

The dissatisfaction seems a bit surprising, given the ease with which associations can make employment information available electronically. The open-ended comments from the survey, however, indicate that some associations are thought to be dominated by senior managers who do not want the association to become a marketplace where competitors can easily lure away their younger employees.

With respect to benefits to the field, the under-30 age group differs significantly from other age groups on three of the 12 benefits. The following table, for example, shows how value perceptions of the youngest and oldest groups differ.

| | Rank Order of Importance | |
|---|---|---|
| **Benefits to the Field** | **Youngest (under 30)** | **Eldest (60 or over)** |
| Supporting student education and entry into the field | 1 | 9 |
| Promoting greater public awareness of contributions in the field | 3 | 6 |
| Maintaining a code of ethics for practice | 5 | 2 |

Understandably, "supporting student education" has great value to the youngest respondents because the memory of this need remains fresh in their minds. "Supporting entry into the field," however, may require new approaches on the part of associations.

As for "promoting greater public awareness of contributions in the field," the entry-level group may be extremely proud of the profession they entered and have greater expectations of the public's acknowledgement. On the other hand, the elders have perhaps learned that the public is not all that interested in any profession, at least not at the level entrants might hope for.

The different rankings for "maintaining a code of ethics" may reflect different levels of temptation at various points in a career. Perhaps temptation does not affect entry-level professionals as menacingly as it does those who have accumulated enough authority to make unethical efforts seem worthwhile. Power and the need for ethics may simply correlate.

# Recommendations

- Monitor the openness with which your association approaches the employment marketplace. If the association restricts access to job postings and career development information, it risks being considered unprofessional as well as not valuable to entry-level professionals.

- Assess your association's approach to welcoming newcomers into the profession and supporting their need for education. Is it based on the idea that only older members have wisdom to impart? For example, mentoring typically involves senior members of the profession helping to orient those just entering the field. Maybe the mentors should come instead from the under-30 group that most recently crossed over into the professional ranks. They may know less about the long-haul requirements, but they appear more interested in the cause and may have a fresher view on career development.

- Consider creating a career-stage spectrum for exploring the various types of ethical situations that an association's members may encounter at different points in their careers. Emphasizing ethics before its utility becomes clear—for example, to entry-level professionals—may appear as mere proselytizing on the association's part.

# CHAPTER 5

# The Quest for International Status

S OME ASSOCIATIONS HAVE BECOME truly international in terms of their mission and membership profiles. Others have weighed whether to expand beyond domestic borders and decided to remain secure in their American nameplate and membership focus. Still other associations have pondered the international option indefinitely or have made the move to go global with little to show for the effort. For this last group, *The Decision to Join* study offers some understanding of how expanding an association to include international members can affect the basic value proposition traditionally offered to domestic members.

American-based associations typically employ one of five strategies when attempting to expand their influence and activities beyond U.S. borders.

1. Grow the association by expanding its global reach, providing full membership and access to all benefits on a global scale. This might be thought of as an expansionist marketing strategy.

2. Welcome global members with the clear understanding that the association remains "American" and will continue to set priorities based on the needs of members located in the United States. This strategy might best be described as internationally hospitable but fundamentally American.

3. Accelerate the expansion of a body of knowledge through global information sharing. This strategy typically appeals to associations with a scientific mission and little concern for border-based competition.

4. Advance the interests of the association's American members through participation in global forums, where access to markets is a primary concern. This describes the strategy of an association whose members are steadfastly American but need a strong advocate to represent their interests in global decisions such as standards setting.

5. Assist developing nations by sharing the expertise of American members. This is first and foremost a philanthropic strategy.

The risk of alienating a domestic membership varies greatly according to the strategy pursued. For example, a science-based profession made up mainly of academic researchers will likely applaud efforts to improve the seamless nature of an international body of knowledge because, when it comes to knowledge, scientists are expansionists. Engineers, on the other hand, may have a similar instinct to expand their body of knowledge on an international scale but worry more about competition; they may fear such a strategy would simply accelerate the transfer of jobs to rapidly developing nations. Technical standard setting associations may want to facilitate a seamless web of complementary standards that support global technologies. Yet, at the same time, the globalization of standards has sent many associations scrambling to protect their intellectual property and market relevance.

## Divergent Priorities

Findings from the survey show that international members—defined as "residing outside the United States," regardless of citizenship—are distinctly different from domestic members in how they rank four benefits to the field.

These rating differences make perfect sense and are worth in-depth consideration if the association makes growth outside the United States a strategic objective. For example, providing standards that support quality has lower importance for those residing outside the United States, probably because the global influence of United States standards varies greatly and because unified European-based standard setting organizations have grown in influence. Maintaining a code of ethics and influencing legislation are also less important

# Ranking Membership Benefits by Location

| Personal Benefits | USA | Outside USA |
|---|:---:|:---:|
| Access to the most up-to-date information available | 1 | 1 |
| Professional development or educational program offerings | 2 | 3 |
| Opportunities to network with other professionals in the field | 3 | 2 |
| Access to career information and employment opportunities | 4 | 5 |
| Access to products, services, and suppliers | 5 | 4 |
| Opportunities to gain leadership experience | 6 | 6 |
| A reference directory of members/practitioners | 7 | 8 |
| Member discounts or group purchasing activities | 8 | 7 |

| Benefits to the Field | USA | Outside USA |
|---|:---:|:---:|
| Providing standards or guidelines that support quality | 1 | 3 |
| Maintaining a code of ethics for practice | 2 | 7 |
| Influencing legislation and regulations that affect the field | 3 | 11 |
| Gathering, analyzing, and publishing data on trends in the field | 4 | 1 |
| Promoting a greater appreciation of the role and value of the field among practitioners | 5 | 5 |
| Promoting greater public awareness of contributions in the field | 6 | 4 |
| Conducting research on significant issues affecting the field | 7 | 2 |
| Supporting student education and entry into the field | 8 | 8 |
| Certifying those who meet critical competency standards | 9 | 9 |
| Attracting competent people into the field | 10 | 6 |
| The association's role in defining critical competencies | 11 | 10 |
| Providing awards or recognition for excellence in the field | 12 | 12 |

to those outside the United States, almost certainly due to variations in how nations frame and enforce ethics and enact legislation. On the other hand, international members express a greater interest in having the association conduct research on significant issues and publish trends-related data.

Although it may come as no surprise to associations with a large international membership, members who reside outside of the United States volunteer at a slightly higher rate than domestic members. The nature of their volunteer activity, however, differs significantly.

**Types of Volunteer Activity by Location**

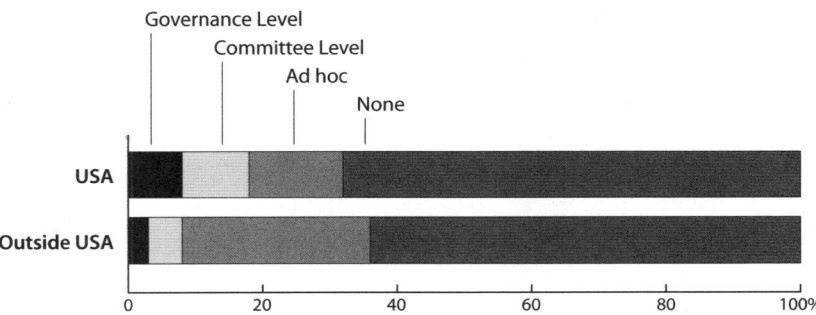

As shown above, ad hoc volunteer participation (such as speaking, writing, presenting, or reviewing content) is higher among respondents who reside outside the United States. Members living in the United States are more likely to report governance- or committee-level volunteering in the previous year.

## Recommendations

- If your association is considering a global strategy, fully analyze the motives driving the decision and what objectives a global strategy will serve. Domestic members may see international initiatives as potentially weakening the association's focus on their needs—or worse, giving global competitors access to association assets that strengthen their position at the expense of the domestic members who generated those assets.

- Clearly articulate the association's motives for embarking on an international strategy, and continue communicating with domestic members as the strategy unfolds. Continually emphasize the association's ongoing allegiance to domestic members.

- Offer myriad opportunities for ad hoc volunteer involvement, especially to members living outside of the United States. Such volunteer activities, which can often be accomplished electronically, also offer opportunities for networking, which global members rank higher on the list of membership benefits than do their domestic counterparts.

- Research and analyze the differences between your international and domestic members. How differently do they value the association's benefits? Do they face similar or vastly different challenges? Determine how much influence international members will have on the association's priority setting and how that influence may affect the satisfaction of domestic members.

# *Closing Thoughts (Including Board Exercise)*

T*HE DECISION TO JOIN* research offers association executives and elected leaders much food for thought. In addition to the five key points outlined in the Introduction, these specific findings carry universal importance for associations:

- The most fundamental driver of an association's appeal to young professionals is the particular needs of their career stage. Those needs tend to endure from one generation to the next, rather than changing according to unique peculiarities identified by generational demographers.

- Association governing structures are dominated by elders, who may not understand that entry-level people place a different value on the various benefits of association membership.

- Uninvolved members are quite similar to former members in how they value the benefits of association membership. Getting those uninvolved members to help in just a small way, through an ad hoc task, can provide a segue to long-term involvement and deeper loyalty.

## A Simple Exercise to Stimulate Board Discussion

Here's a simple, five-step exercise to help facilitate a useful discussion of the key points covered in this monograph. The best time to do this might be as part of an annual meeting in which board members consider the association's strategic priorities for the next fiscal year.

1. Ask all board members to read this monograph in advance of the meeting, taking time to consider the importance of the five key points as they relate to the association's management culture and operating assumptions.

2. Before the meeting begins, ask each board member to place the five key points in rank order of importance. For example, if you believe that the association should emphasize the collective benefits of membership, then rank that point as "1." If the association has no international ambitions, then rank that point as "5." This ranking can be done using a simple paper form, or board members can enter their data into a spreadsheet on a laptop at the board meeting.

3. After collecting the data, use a simple spreadsheet to analyze the results. In the following table, the first column contains the five points in their short

form. The next series of columns enable each board member to record his or her rankings; this example assumes 12 board members. The next column calculates an average score using the function =AVERAGE(B2:M2), adjusting "M" to agree with the column generated by the number of board members. These numbers are used to determine the overall rankings as shown in column "O," where the lowest average score indicates the top overall ranking. The last column calculates a standard deviation, which can be used to determine the level of divergent thinking, or degree of like-mindedness, among board members. The function for this is =STDEV(B2:M2).

| Key Points | Individual Board Member Rankings | | | | | | | | | | | | Average Scores | Rankings | STDEV |
|---|---|---|---|---|---|---|---|---|---|---|---|---|---|---|---|
| A | B | C | D | E | F | G | H | I | J | K | L | M | N | O | P |
| Perceptions of Benefits | 2 | 4 | 1 | 4 | 3 | 2 | 4 | 3 | 3 | 4 | 3 | 1 | 2.83 | 2 | 1.11 |
| Value of Involvement | 1 | 2 | 3 | 3 | 1 | 4 | 3 | 4 | 2 | 5 | 2 | 3 | 2.75 | 1 | 1.22 |
| Leader v. Member Perceptions | 4 | 1 | 2 | 5 | 4 | 3 | 5 | 5 | 1 | 3 | 4 | 2 | 3.25 | 5 | 1.48 |
| Generational Differences | 5 | 3 | 5 | 2 | 2 | 1 | 2 | 2 | 4 | 1 | 5 | 4 | 3.00 | 3 | 1.54 |
| Quest for International Status | 3 | 5 | 4 | 1 | 5 | 5 | 1 | 1 | 5 | 2 | 1 | 5 | 3.17 | 4 | 1.85 |

(Sum each column to verify accuracy.)

4. Distribute the spreadsheet analysis and start the discussion with the top-ranked item: *Why did we rank this point number 1, and what should we do to change or at least question our assumptions?* Allocate about 20 minutes to discuss the top-ranked point, followed by 15 minutes for the second-ranking point, and 10 minutes for each of the subsequent points. If the results in column "P" indicate divergent thinking among board members, consider addressing that as well: *Why are our rankings so varied on this point? If you gave it a high ranking, please explain why. If you gave it a low ranking, please explain why.*

5. Generate some tangible outcomes. Be creative in addressing the specific assumptions operating in your association's environment. For example, if board members agree that the association needs to address its international status, the outcome may be, "Conduct ongoing focus group research to track domestic members' perceptions of international strategies and identify the most effective ways to communicate." Or, if what's most important is closing the gap between leadership and rank-and-file perceptions, the outcome may be: "Build this point into the annual orientation of new board members, emphasizing the need to communicate more effectively when these differences are understood and inevitable." Or it may read, "Obtain better data so board members are not making decisions based on insufficient marketing data or outdated member needs analyses."

## Time Requirements

| | |
|---|---|
| Read the monograph and rank points | 30 minutes |
| Set up spreadsheet to analyze the data | 30 minutes |
| Discuss rankings and generate outcomes | 60 minutes |
| Total Time: | 2 Hours |

# Additional Reading and Programs

*The Volunteer Leadership Issue of Associations Now,* published annually by ASAE & The Center for Association Leadership.

*Enhancing Committee Effectiveness: Handbook for Committee Chairs, Staff Liaisons, and Committee Members, 2nd Edition,* by Jack Schlegel, 2009, ASAE & The Center for Association Leadership.

*Governing for Growth: Using 7 Measures of Success to Strengthen Board Dialogue and Decision Making,* 2009, ASAE & The Center for Association Leadership.

*7 Measures of Success: What Remarkable Associations Do That Others Don't,* 2006, ASAE & The Center for Association Leadership.

*7 Measures of Success Implementation Guide & Assessment Tool,* 2008, ASAE & The Center for Association Leadership.

*The Decision to Join: How Individuals Determine Value and Why They Choose to Belong,* by James Dalton and Monica Dignam, 2007, ASAE & The Center for Association Leadership.

In addition to other programs, ASAE & The Center for Association Leadership offer two programs dedicated to helping teams of chief executive officers and chief elected officers enhance the board's performance. Visit www.asaecenter.org/programsevents for the latest calendar and list of programs.

# *About the Author*

**James Dalton,** president of Strategic Counsel, is a management consultant to the nonprofit community with specialties in customer research, process improvement, strategic planning, and leadership development. Prior to establishing his consulting practice, Dalton served as chief executive officer of the American Society of Landscape Architects, where he instituted an ongoing member research program to gather information on member satisfaction, changing market dynamics, and emerging issues that define the needs of the profession. He also spent 18 years at the National Society of Professional Engineers, where he served in a number of roles including that of deputy executive director. Dalton has been an active volunteer in ASAE & The Center for Association Leadership and has acted as a primary author and contributor on the topic of strategic planning and leadership. His works include *From Scan to Plan: Managing*

*Change in Associations* and *From Scan to Plan: Integrating Trends into the Strategy-Making Process,* and he coauthored *The Decision to Join: How Individuals Determine Value.* He was a member of ASAE & The Center's Measures of Success Task Force, whose multi-year efforts resulted in the landmark *7 Measures of Success: What Remarkable Associations Do That Others Don't,* published in 2006. Previously, as a member of the ASAE Foundation Research Committee, he served as liaison to the Wharton School on a collaborative project investigating the strategy-making process in associations.